THE HOUSE OF WOLVES

Poems by
Brian K. Turner

BLUE LIGHT PRESS ◆ 1ST WORLD PUBLISHING

1ST WORLD
PUBLISHING

SAN FRANCISCO ◆ FAIRFIELD ◆ DELHI

The House of Wolves

Copyright ©2020 Brian K. Turner

BLUE LIGHT PRESS
www.bluelightpress.com
bluelightpress@aol.com

1ST WORLD PUBLISHING
PO Box 2211
Fairfield, IA 52556
www.1stworldpublishing.com

BOOK & COVER DESIGN
Melanie Gendron
melaniegendron999@gmail.com

INTERIOR ILLUSTRATION
"Moon Wolf" © 2000 Melanie Gendron

AUTHOR PHOTO
César Love

FIRST EDITION

ISBN: 978-1-4218-3678-2

The House of Wolves

Table of Contents

Alleys and Parking Lots

I just happened to be there to witness a small cat chasing drifting feathers in a downtown parking lot, too immersed in living to even know he didn't have a home. Debates of well-intentioned mission or vulgar intrusion aside, I pondered a course to follow ...

It reminded me of all the lessons I never learned from my father, who gushed that you only help the weak if you are soft, help the abandoned if you are lost, and only feel pain if you're not inflicting it.

His parish was a growling scimitar of rabid dogs, chasing the brightness away from every living corner. Great black-winged birds flooded his stillborn sky, all set on a canvas of simmering rage, its sullen closed-mouth colors forever on the prowl for carefree joy.

A frigid, wind-swept bay of half-light was a safe nursery for the dogs to roam, but ceaseless winters bred only black full moons that no longer commanded echoes of trenchant howling. And so the many passing years softened the beasts, and finally on a warm spring night, they quietly turned down a dank back alley and disappeared.

Letting go of his mad imaginings and his puerile curses was as close to peace as he'd find, and I, witnessing the last shadowed flickers of light dowsed from him in this air of bleeding dust, was as close to understanding as I would ever know ...

And if I had not brought home the rain-sparkled kitten from the downtown parking lot, my soul would not be worth the paper it's bleeding on

Moments in Ice

Her hand was light in its expression,
    coolly sweeping the salty air with casual cigarette held aloft

Her voice was cool like amber on the terrace
    where we dared the world to call us mortal

We lingered in soft embrace, thinking that if the
    silence stretched long enough we would melt together

The pregnant wave bursting on a waiting shore
    made a grand gesture, I thought, watching the frail mist
        chase her smile across a forever seagull morning …

Her fingers carelessly flicked ashes
    amidst the furious logic of explaining goodbye

Her voice was cool like amber
    in the café where I wouldn't dare make a scene

I lingered in my protest, thinking that if the words
    stretched long enough, we could still die together

The cigarette raised again and glowed
    like an obscene exclamation

The purse swinging gracefully off the table and over a shoulder
    made a grand gesture, I thought,
        watching the frail blue smoke
            chasing her words across a forever starling twilight

Carving the Mystic Wood

Night has dreamt away its thick and fleshy blackness,
　　　　and the Humboldt morning bleeds its cold affliction
　　　　　　　　on a rocky sunless shore
The moon is a harlot to its faithful tides,
　　　　　　racing the sky as the water churns blindly
　　　　　　　　　　towards the husk of pearly scent

Redwood sentinels guard the fog-drowned coast,
　　　　　impaling the humming sky like mad infected steeples
　　　　Hidden aloft, spotted owls glow coolly
　　　　　　　with the gift of fatal vision
The succulent fever of life burns slowly in this cathedral;
　　　　the woods are dank and redolent,
　　　　　　　simmering in the lungs to the edge of bursting
But part the tall canopy and you'll see the cancer:
　　　　malignant roadways winding to the heart of the marrow
　　　　　　with the low rumble of men

We wander the cool loam drunken in your shadows,
　　　　straining for your sigh, but lamenting mostly
　　　　that our deaths come dull and lingering like a tepid mist
But your death, my friend, is a prideful beast,
　　　　with a face of headlights,
　　　　　　steely teeth,
　　　　　　　　and the fecund breath of diesel

Trees are silent martyrs of a secret council,
　　　　breeding slender faith motionless
　　　　　against the gathering whispers of storm
So guard the coast in your dwindling hours
　　　　with your back pressed against the sea;
　　　　I will think of you often in the barrenness,

3

the fleeting touch of your eager skin,
your cool, moist breath,
and how you made love with the fog
through the window
until, at last,
you became the dark and fleshy night

(Coast redwood: <u>Sequoia sempervirens</u>)

Bitter Spring
(Donner Party, 1846)

The crippled sky moans low over Donner Pass —
    the sinuous, hungry phantom
        with the icy breath of lions,
            crouched in its lair with eyes watchful
                for imperious voyagers

A virgin party set forth bearing
    crosses for the sun,
      then was swallowed whole within starved whimpers of prayer,
        and the Truckee Lake landscape bloomed with
           gnawed bones in the following bitter spring

The mountains hold their ghosts dearly,
      with a loving clench
        stretching prone and silent
          across the grey, motionless tapestry

Even summer here bares gleaming teeth,
    languid and waiting among the firs until nightfall,
      panting low with a nervous growl
Aspens soon warn of the coming hunger with
      a sudden yellow scream,
        withering to a sullen red
            on the cusp of season's twilight

Winter dreams deeply without color,
    throwing its icy blanket on
      the restless, heaving granite
        straining skyward

The Pass considers its prey
  with a cunning silence,
   blinking slyly with a clear morning,
    poised, stalking,
     then the whispering snow tucks you slowly in
      with a tender madness —
     the soft,
      gentle,
       cannibal snow

Lividity

There are ghost ships burning across a dull-eyed sky
    with blood and satisfaction
Flaming timbers burst, and the shard memories
      tumble carelessly through the dimming half-light
       of our heart's once bountiful landscape

Once-treasured moments are now relic islands,
    separated by sullen latitudes and quietly receding
         under grey blanket tides.
Your gravity releases me;
    I float like a distant moon
      scarcely interrupting your sky,
    as you repose beneath in soft, erotic gardens

My beast is caged once more,
    now mute and sessile — only the eyes still ravenous.
In cypress twilight, my dreams think of
       wandering your garden, searching and
    finding you and reaching you — almost.
But there in frail blue mist I stop and coil;
    with trepid gaze holding barely on,
      gently plucking the slim shadowed roses
        of your graveyard smile

One After Zero

There's a certain half-remembered place somewhere;
it can be found, they say, in the tombs of a half-buried
castle, nestled in the soft, shadowed crevice
of a supple neckline.

But that's not where you're headed …

In a half-forgotten place, a jagged-tooth ingress
is looming, spattered lightly in blood; the remnants of a
cold, aural dissonance lapping at your feet in a gentle tide.

What dogma trail did you follow to finally lose the sun,
and find only hearts too timorous to even beat aloud?
A legion of stolid citizens who never smelled a battlefield,
yet are eager to ship off their neighbors' sons and daughters
to spurt angry blood in someplace they couldn't
find on a map because, stupid, war is good for business.
You may know these meritorious patriots:
They're called America.

And what fallow vines bear fruit for me?
They've left me behind, or mock me in their slavering death
masks. It's O.K., that's the least of my problems.
I must qualify, at least to the post-mortem revisionists,
for the vivisection necessary to achieve my moral equanimity.

To that I am sentenced, still attempting to collect debts
from the dank marrow of long-forgotten dead men.

Plague Angels

There is curious refuge for you in
 restless prairie winds, gazing on
departing mother smiling faintly back
from the worn yellow photos

Her disease was cool and spoke
at night with tremulous voice;
it loved and stroked her from the soft
familiar glow of amber glass

Your eyes bleed gentle memories
of arctic terns fleeing a stark winter moon

Black and white Polaroid trembles —
a child with a hand perched sparrow-like on the trim shoulder

Patient death grins at photo's
spurious immortality
Marrow of life bursts an exodus from
bone, viscera, and skin towards the sanity
of dust.
Solemn earth reclaims the gifts
offered at birth

Relent at last, let the smiling
plague angels ascend your night of dream,
closing hard doors on the wilting half-measures
of the soft hand's fading blush

Entropy

I have lost your opal moon in my smoke-ravaged sky.
Tattooed vows melt on the canceled face of a slate promontory,
forming pastel rivulets meandering seaward.
Relic horses wander the moonless beach;
listless waves bleed upon the sullen, zodiac shore.

I am my own transgression, with bad karma and
snake venom coursing through the roiling blood,
but better to betray you than to bore you.

I imagine your scorn like God's bitter kiss
on the brows of the doomed garden crows.

You are at last your own forgiveness,
and I float uselessly amid the dark sculptures of memory,
past the flashpoint of my entropy, voiceless and blind
among the tall spires of your erotic chaos.

Aphonia

In morning mist you breech our invisible door with
softly predatory guile.
Scan the landscape of your dominion, the perpetual
winter of a grey forgotten field.
Through a warped glass your stoic plastic Jesus
stares densely at the mourning doves wilting
on the wire.

Summer has long misplaced our broken, halting steps,
but I miss the moment of awkward dance,
the deft turn of gaze, your politely disenfranchised eyes
simmering with mordant song.

But your vision is without touch —
now, twilight receding, giving away at last a
fleeting, resolute smile...
A bit like that time you fell into slumber and
disappeared behind the shadow of my purgatory sky...

Her faded blossom eyes too eagerly discarded their song —
And what of her dreams?
Nothing left but the bones and feathers.

Notes from the Orphan Asylum, 1879

The blood-drained beast rises Citadel-like above the
    vast Ohio landscape
Hand prints stain the clinging, predatory walls

Shadows conceal nothing; hard floors still creak softly in
    dark abeyance
Mute pleas yearn even for a grey, stillborn December sky;
      another sated winter throws its tattered wool blanket across
        icy muffled cries

The crippled voices dissolve into a ragged aphasia —
    with faint echoes redolent of
        tuberculosis,
            black karma, and
                rigid, skeleton gates

Graves toil in endless rows, pulsing skyward —
      All are neatly numbered, bereft of names
The stolid keepers know the noise of command;
    only rivers and constellations need names
Hickory trees faintly whisper the souls in their
    feathery April plumage

Seasons stretch into dark legacy —
    Ancient limestone towers, strangely proud,
      hold their breath while embracing the huddled ghosts
        with grim devotion

In a dusty corner of strewn rubble a sad witness
    holds dark secrets —
A one-eyed doll, with crooked grin and distant,
    time-frozen gaze …

Someone once gave her a name

Casual Infirmities

What a grave burden to you, this unwanted love of mine,
with no mantel space to hold it, so the sticky
residue settles on the floor in useless, tepid pools

Instead, your piercing, color-swept eyes
wash clean the laurel trees in pristine
self-loathing rivers, and your cemetery dogs
lie sleeping in bleached October winds

I imagine someday you'll forgive a fortunate soul's
transgression of love, but you're not what matters
anymore, I suppose, floating wistfully in
naked, distant skies

I don't mind the gashes anymore, but please
exempt the world your sad, pious birds of vengeance —
the brooding gulls seduced to patrol
an empty seascape of dawn

I can't help a final time but to finger
the love as burning wax that drips a muddled fog
across your sweet, mute winter trees

You owe us nothing

Prowl

Soft paw prints we leave as evidence
    in the cool forest loam as we tire, chased
Weaving path of darkness in partnered crime of stolen destiny,
                our larceny of fate —
        and world-encroaching verdict awaits

To prowl with you, my mate,
   in our blinding moment of life
Hot breath shared, panting
    Soft fur, wet, mingling
Pause in the cool clutch of this dank infested night

   Stealth
      Stalk
         Poise
           Leap

Seize the throat in a crushing blow
   Share the kill
      Devour the night,
    its bone shards scattered
Howl to the hills,
     to the pale moon witness passing,
    emboldened in moment of silver triumph

But we tire, chased, the dog pack's jaws dripping hard

I taste your hunger, salty sweat fear,
    wounds gently seeping, sticky and warm
   Our eyes meet fixed in silent consultation —
        Agreed:
      Roam, one final time —
         Face the hunters

Thirst unending over ancient stream bent,
     gazing from the ribs of canyon refuge
         to the forest crouched and grinning
A soft gurgle in the throat
       as the hunt pants closer

Now,
  fangs bared, gleaming —
      Enter the arena
    Cool exile of dream abandoned,
      Earth jaws awaiting our end
Final look exchanged, knowing
     To perish untamed,
       destiny shackled;
      the gold arrows are waiting,
        and red eyes surround us in the forest
           through our final prowl of night

Lycanthropy

We are no longer the panorama
                of a limitless landscape
We have grown small and distant
    We prowl beneath different suns now,
                and worship different moons

We have lost our funny language
    My howls are silent to you now,
        and no more raise fur in the blank turn
            of your cool repose

I prowl our distant meadow
    and seek you among the twisted oaks,
        then perch upon the sandstone altar
            where once we chased a glorious chaos
                of verdant rapture and scented madness

I will have to linger and be crazy alone
        and chant my moonrise spell in silence now,
      shivering in the endless twilight
        of your cool reason

The Infamy and Notoriety of Old Litigious Coyotes

And so I lost you —
    I never thought the chasm would endure ...

Plans, plans, plans
    Coolly deliberating the calculus of penitence
    and redemption;
breeding slender faith trembling like a cat's
    desolate shadow on the wall.
The useless letters I prayed would be a road map home —
    Grammar, diction, syntax, metaphor, simile:
    mere blackwater typhoid lagoons.

Onward home alone now, bustling through a rogue gallery
    of rabid cockroaches, and a few insolent yet worldly
    crickets fixed on the mildew walls.
Perhaps the puckish starlings will wistfully recall
    our final twisted stroll together, with a gentle snow
    rending small, frozen holes in our unraveling comfort.

Taking baby steps as a recovering romantic —
    betting with Confederate money in a duel with
    the horrid gatekeeper in lace, while courting the
    slow bloodless cancer of infinite grey hours
    to nowhere.

And so I lost you —
    Tormented by gateless pleasures I never
    earned nor could afford ...

Perhaps I can still die well,
    though parched, colorless, and unforgiven.

I can always hope

Indentured Solitude

I don't even recall saying my goodbyes, but the velvet tier of rain clouds were unforgiving, expelling all the songbirds we once knew by name, and the resulting acrid silence rendered tarry blackness to all awkward flickers of verse.

There is, it seems, rarely a stark wild urgency for love, merely a tamed and neutered yearning to not die in its absence. Our sacred vows, much like everyone's, were meant only to convince ourselves, then crudely etched in wax beneath an equatorial sun. But in emotive pestilence a stockyard of sad memories wait fitfully for their conquest of birth, sourly gestating within our forlorn "Can we give it one last try?"

So were the silent songs of distant caverns what we miss more than those actually given voice? And where were the tormented starlings when we needed them most? Awash in mares' blood blindly encircling indifferent, rakish moons.

Many a night I dreamed, or cursed full-throatedly, a roguish midnight luxuriating in the drunken wallow of a bleary, infirm loathing of love and self.

And somewhere in that vexed fragrant evening I ventured into throbbing sleep convinced some silken future would still awaken me, only to stiffly emerge in grey tawdry sheets poleaxed on the encasement of an amber past, and the past just ain't what they promised it would be.

So great aspirations seem always to succumb to venal lust, but finally, it seems, I can lay claim to that grand failure that has always eluded me.

I can no longer court the bloodless seas of wayward skies drowning beneath the smoldering gulls — these are merely the sickly grey roots spawning in our sodden, idiot perdition.

Dear God I miss her quiet, tragic comforts.

Livid Spring

I may not believe in God,
                but I still curse Him

To live and die is to question —
How many questions will still fester in twilight,
and how much time will death afford you to mutely muse
all the useless answers?

My forlorn question to you is how do I know you —
To know every one of your sad-eyed, hollow heartbeats,
and to hold each as a slowly strangling sparrow?

Dogs are unnerved when challenged with
changes in geniality;
Cats regard insanity as just another form of play ...

Carrying buckets across the river,
there are indeed wan finishings —
The anomie of your acquiescence sweetly waxing on the wing;
The exuberant melancholy of your last timorous wave ashore.
Finally, a grey symphony of blood bleating
through the hard-packed morning of snow.

We, unlike cats, will welcome the grace and ardor
of cooperative graves.
We all, in time I pray, will embrace the
frantic politesse of insanity.

Oh, who cares; we will probably simply languish
in the fragrant vomitous of rabid coyotes.

We all die invisible.

Blood Moon

Eyes of ghost children wanly scan a burning field.
Eyes like distant farm houses.
Eyes pleading like dogs in winter.

The Norman Rockwell family farms of a dead-and-gone
Americana fade from the prairie canvas,
nibbled sweetly by locusts of the agri-combine co-op factory,
locusts descending from brilliant free trade skies,
tirelessly munching beneath a mute bucolic sun.

Under a wolf moon, feckless winds covet bleeding casts
of dry milo, which will be cleared for the new mutant race,
engineered by shareholder bison grazing un-yoked.

Now foreclosed is our golden wave tomorrow.
The children look back at last, through the fallow myth
of wide-eyed pioneer snapshots.
Light prisms twist the memories in cruel refractions
to the corner of the barn where the stillborn foal
lay frozen through the long forgotten February.

Winter Harvest

The clouds advanced in grey legions with a sullen leer,
    then perished in plump droplets beyond the terrace,
        each one scarring its tiny legacy on the
            parched meadow spreading out from
                the foot of the stairs

A child, trapped by glass, watched his mother in furious effort
    to save the laundry skewered on the line. The rescue
      complete, the wet bundle was assembled around
          the hearth, like us safe and warm.
But later that night, the roads became icy reapers on the prowl,
    and this became his first memory of winter,
         and his last memory of mother

And in the final meandering brush strokes of an artist's
    rendering of a life, the cracked child looks back through
         the clouds with dust and longing

Better Left Unsaid

The leper colony have implanted childhood memories for you,
to more comfortably assure you of being alive.
The drifting bones of sickly clouds trickle meager daylight
on the rummaged terrace outside your old nursery.
Tears creep down the fingers of your eyes like ripe bodies
in bloated rivers, whispering echoes of the deaf.

Resting languidly on a bed of fresh skulls, the undisciples
of partial truths nearly convinced me to watch a television.
I'm content to bathe in their opprobrium, and not seek
punitive recourse against the cockroaches I met in my
kitchen.

Headless mannequins topple gleefully through stairwells and
courtyards. In torrents they shop for your curtains with
the cobwebs already sewn in to save time; old, faded portraits
talk you down from the walls.

All the while, sentries of your mutant nightmares hunt down
the crippled effigies that just wouldn't burn.   Now, you blithely
walk into forever with a lyric smile wilting slightly in
methodical sorrow — I will try sleeping beneath your tongue
in trite, swollen libido.

Don't blame me; take the reins from the social champagne
cocktailers who stalk you. They could only love you — I can
curse and bleed for you.

I am no longer staring into the abyss, the abyss is smiling
into me, confidently insisting that I never was ...

This

This is how it ends …

Two wolves circling, cornering wounded love in closed arena,
slavering for a chance to seize the throat —
    and children inside clawing to get out,
    with screams unheard above the howling

Two crippled children flailing at the darkness,
    the darkness in each other;
    each pushing down the drowning child with a
    terrible precision, long into the cool clutches
    of this dank infested night

This is not how it was born —

Remember the race through verdant fields,
    fingering a moon tethered by tides in the pregnant
    overflow of fevered dance like rare Nile insects
We prowled the meadows and carved the hills alive,
    daring the judgment of sea headlong into the fluid clench
    of soft, shadowed willows

But this is how it ends —

My disease whispering softly with yours, conspiring, rejoined;
    your disease complying gently with mine, dead staring eyes
    holding cold affliction poised for a slaying

Slow ticking of long sojourn of plague
    In a lunge I strike your heart, your mirrored heart of mine
In a whirl you return it intact,
    exchanging howls of starched lunatic moon

Scarred pale dawn emerges at last, crouched curious
over viscera of jagged splintered night …

This is the death of the child at last
This is blood that won't wash out of our memory
This is dreading the cold fabric of night alone
This is dying alone without love
This is love wailing under black rail yard skies

So this is how it ends …

This is me saying I love you with roses of drying tears
This is me saying I love you far too late
This is me saying I love you anyway

This is me saying I love you

Succinct Verse

1.

Bare chestnut trees,
dry swimming pool swollen with leaves,
and April sleeps within a future moon

2.

Under moon of woven silk,
the sinuous white cat
curls up against the sated winter

3.

Lightning cries above the marsh;
from the darkness, life is frozen
in the strobe flash of a heron's wing

4.

Like phantom water,
the cougar pours himself
across our dark unknown

5.

Faded dresses lay folded in the box —
through the smeared window
she eyes the past with dust and envy

Succinct Verse

6.

Mist-shrouded horses wander a moonless beach
Hooves sink below resilient waves,
daring the blind tide to retrace its steps

7.

A dragonfly alights —
the marsh quivers, and becomes
his cloak of studied silence

8.

Winter seizes the knave young river —
the callow ice cracks with yearning
Beyond the sky, patient sea smiles in wait

9.

Restless sea turns in its sleep
The pinto mare, prisoner of shore,
will mourn the drowning moon

Succinct Verse

11.

Inside the cramped broom closet,
The mouse's heart races; his eyes glow alive —
Outside, the sinuous cat knows how to wait

12.

The storm paws him roughly,
but the stallion recalls the saddle,
and doesn't mind

13.

The wolf's fur raises, uncertain —
Ghosts he never knew
warn him of teak arrows

15.

A slight rustling in snowy branches:
No one can trace the night voice
but the owl who abandoned it

Succinct Verse

21.

Faint rustlings rise through the snow —
The mouse will soon find out
what the fox above already knows

22.

The buck crashes down with shattered neck;
he bleeds softly in dream of his mate,
but the bullet has the final say

23.

The whale breaches in daring leap
from one sphere to another —
water, sky, then back again to silence

24.

The lynx awakens at night to packed snow
Blinking hard, she finds her footing,
and the winter hunt begins

25.

From the distant night sky,
the owl sees a sharp outline —
a form the field mouse never knew he had

About the Author

B rian was born into Scorpio on a cold November evening in a prior century. He grew up in California with a fascination for nature, wildlife and especially the ocean. After high school he worked a series of manual labor positions, various and nondescript. He enlisted in the Army in 1991 during the build-up to Desert Storm. Somehow he attained the rank of Sergeant and served as a gunner on a M1A1 tank.

Following military service he returned to California and eventually earned a Master of Science degree in Environmental Science from California State University, Fullerton, a degree he has never applied to any practical use. For years after he worked in animal sanctuaries helping rehabilitate exotic animals rescued from abusive environments. Currently he operates his own facility helping domestic and exotic animals recover from abuse and abandonment. Any animal that has passed away from old age or infirmity is buried on the property and visited every evening. Brian is a born-again heretic and an avowed neo-Marxist.

Brian K. Turner's literary interests began by reading the work of Edgar Allan Poe when he was a young person. He attended creative writing classes at California State University, Hayward with Don Markos, a renowned poet from Piraeus, Greece. When attending California State University, Hayward, he was invited to read at the Hayward Arts Council auditorium. He has read at cafés in San Francisco, Castro Valley, and Dublin, California. He was a featured reader in the *Haight Ashbury Literary Journal*'s readings at the Sacred Grounds Café and the BEAT Museum in San Francisco. He has been invited twice by the California Geographical Society to read at the "John Muir Festival" during their annual symposium at Yosemite National Park.

Brian K. Turner has had fifty publications in thirty-six different literary magazines. Some of these include *Occam's*

Razor (California State University, Hayward), *Lucidity* (Bear House Publishing), *Direction* (Los Angeles Pierce College), *Voicings from the High Country* (Casper, Wyoming), *The Storyteller*, *Haight Ashbury Literary Journal*, *Bear Creek Haiku*, *Hiram Poetry Review*, *Tiger's Eye*, *Love's Chance*, and *The Lives of Artists* from Dance of My Hands Publishing. His poetry is included in the Inkwell Press' *Anthology* from Mesa, Arizona. He has been published internationally in *Poetic Hours* from Erran Publishing, Nottingham, England, in *First Time* from East Sussex, England, *Pennine Ink* from Burnley, Great Britain, *The Eclectic Muse* from Richmond, Canada, as well as in Australia.

Acknowledgements

"Alleys and Parking Lots" *Hiram Poetry Review* Spring 2018 Issue # 79. *Haight Ashbury Literary Journal* Fall 2018 Vol.34 no. 1, *Conceit* March 2018, Vol. 11 no.132, *Blue Unicorn*, Fall 2018 Vol. XLII no.1, *Pennine Ink* 2018 Issue 40

"Moments in Ice" *Lucidity* (Bear House Publishing) Summer 2000 Vol.15 #1, *Anthology* (Inkwell Press) Nov-Dec 2000 Vol. VII no.6, *Poetic Hours* Autumn 2005 Issue no.25 *Offerings* Fourth Qt. 2005 Vol. XII no. 4, *Northern Stars* Sept/Oct. 2015, *Conceit* March 2018 Vol. 11 no.132, *Awakenings Review* Fall 2018 Vol. 7 no. 2, *The Eclectic Muse* Vol. 15 2009

"Carving the Mystic Wood" *Anthology* (Inkwell Press) Nov-Dec 2000 Vol. VII no.6, *Hidden Oak* Spring Summer/ 2005, *Nomad's Chair* Vol. 15 Issue 3 July 2007, *California Quarterly* Autumn 2019 Vol. 45 no. 3, *Northern Stars* Sept/Oct 2015

"Bitter Spring" *The Blind Man's Rainbow* Autumn 2003 Vol. IX Issue 1, *Hidden Oak* Spring/Summer 2005, *Black Book* Sept 2008 Issue no. 42, *Conceit* Jan. 2020 Vol. 13 no. 154

"Lividity" *Small Brushes* April-Sept 2005, *First Time* Autumn 2005-Edition #49

"One After Zero" *Haight Ashbury Literary Journal* 2019 Vol. 35 no. 1, *Conceit* Dec. 2019 Vol. 13 no. 153

"Plague Angels" *Star Poets* July/August 2016, *Haight Ashbury Literary Journal* July/August 2016, *Awakenings Review* Fall 2018 Vol. 7 no. 2, *Conceit* Feb. 2020 Vol. 13 no. 155

"Entropy" *Love's Chance* Summer 2009, *The Storyteller* Vol. 18 Issue 2 April-June 2013

"Aphonia" *Fighting Chance* Fall/Winter 2008, *The Storyteller* Vol. 13 Issue 4 Oct-Dec 2008, *Conceit* March 2018 Vol. 11 no.132

"Notes from the Orphan Asylum, 1879" *Haight Ashbury Literary Journal* Vol. 31, no. 1 2014

"Casual Infirmities" *Poetry Explosion* July 2007, *Love's Chance* Fall/Winter 2008

"Prowl" *Direction 1992*

"Lycanthropy" *Tiger's Eye* Mid-Autumn 2005 Issue no.10, *Hidden Oak* Fall-Winter 2005, *Poetry Explosion* 2015 Vol. no. 102

"Blood Moon" *Abbey* Feb 2015 Issue no.141

"Winter Harvest" *Feelings of the Heart* August-Nov. 2004

"Better Left Unsaid" *Conceit* Jan. 2020 Vol. 13 no. 154

Many of "Succinct Verse" have been published in *Bear Creek Haiku, Poetry Explosion, Northern Stars, The Aurorean,* and *Shemom* from 2012-20

www.ingramcontent.com/pod-product-compliance
Lightning Source LLC
Chambersburg PA
CBHW021916040426
42447CB00007B/894